In the Center of the Eclipse

Stefanie Lea Winton

BookLeaf Publishing

India | USA | UK

Presentation by *BookLeaf Publishing*

Web: www.bookleafpub.com

E-mail: info@bookleafpub.com

ISBN: 9789363318847

First edition 2024

for Cynthia Sperling

143

ACKNOWLEDGEMENT

"Love is a word of light,
written by a hand of light,
upon a page of light."

  Kahlil Gibran

Cover Photograph
by Momma Shalla
April 8 2024

PREFACE

"I am a dream,
this moment is a dream"
    Jack Kerouac

In the Center of the Eclipse;
muse kaleidoscope,
light fragments,
resilience to Aprils Cruelty,
a hope,
a prayer,
a hail mary into infinity,
an Avalon love letter
in gold cursive.
The present moment is eternal.
Illumination.

The Door to the Garden of Light

Eclipse,
evereve dream,
iridescent evergreen iris,
Isis,
indigo inscription,
Cygnus in shadows
& the crescent sun
sharpens into a fiery scythe
in the twilight illusion.

Portal

A door in the ice opens,
& out pours white roses
& moon jellyfish.
Give me one of your secrets,
jagged, deep truth.
Winter glass garden,
dreamworld.
I want to believe
in the enigma of blue.

Bishop Arts District 3/3/24

Live in the heart
of something real;
rosebuds & lightbulbs
& rusty owls,
thistle & lore
& little dogs.
Sunshine & love;
Sundays.

Mist

& the opal
was lost
in the mist
of everything
that once was.
& she sat aside
lavender grey
moonlit roses
& prayed.

Jupiter House

Moonfire Dream Machine,
island of neon stars.
The crystal roots
of lost souls
reach into Eternity.
The spire of desire
rises & spirals in me.
Dare to dream neon red stars.
The lost are found
& carried home.

Atmospheric Heaven

Azure Venus
sets cerulean dawn.
Prometheus rises
from the ashes
of false light angels,
passing the torch
to future souls
lost on the opal planes
of Autumns final sigh.

143

Lake Tahoe blue,
I love you.
At the edge of Avalon,
kiss me in the snow
in the space between
sunset & blue.
Lake Filled Calderas,
Azores,
Island of sapphire dust & dreams
& butterfly wings
carry us to sleep
in the memory of blue,
in the cradle of the sea,
Hydrangea blue,
blue blue blue,
love me in the memory of blue,
forever.

Tulips

I'm tiptoeing through the tulips,
Eternity's shadow cast
on the red brick wall
on the way to Devon Tower.
Rapunzel, Rapunzel,
sunset skyscraper,
blue glass,
Infinity.

Myriad magic,
spring equinox,
on the edge of Eclipse.

Even the Hydrangeas are blooming.
The eve teems with laughter
& sweet delirium madness.
Drunk off sunshine & love.
Kiss me under the red rose bloom
before Time ends.

Moon

Moreover,
onyx eclipsed emerald,
only Angels entered Avalon,
nexus, sweet surrender.

Reincarnation

Moroccan Rose,
butterfly blue,
Nymph at the edge
of an ethereal Elysian River,
evading Pan,
wild Satyr
faded twilight.
My power belongs to me
& me alone
& I will shine
in the shadow of the moon
forever.

Doll Heart

At the edge
of Grand Canyon blue,
she slowly sang

"& someday
you will ache
like I ache"

& the void
echoed solace.

Doorway

"Oh mirror in the sky
what is love?"
        Stevie Nicks

Green and black butterflies
cut from paper dreams
molded melted wax drips
from Sacramento Skies
flying east.
There are spells etched on glass,
rain can never wash away love

44 East

I listened to Coltrane's Blue Train
on the toll road to Tulsa.
I drove two hours to kiss
the Cherry Blossoms Goodnight.
To remind them,
I have not forgotten love.
Lost in a cityscape oasis
on the edge of an eclipse,
keep me the spaces
between butterfly wings,
a mosaic memory of blue.
Heaven blooms indigo
clocks & paper ships burn
like little lanterns & sail away
flaming and wavering.
I want to live
between the heartbeats
when you first fall in love.
Meet me beneath
Dante & Beatrice's window
before the tulips die.
A tale as old as time;
Atlantis, sunken blue.
I love you,
like watching glass

melt in the moonlight.
Keep me in the spaces
between sunlight & sorrow.
Holy Matrimony!
All Artist drown
in jasmine bloomed midnights.
I love you,
like sheet music left in the rain
ink notes smeared into a river
as the melody slips away.

Cusp

I'll keep secrets like I love you
in sleet melting into the tulips
& Spring weeps at Winter's sweeping return.
One last wet kiss.
On the cusp of the eclipse,
Sarah Vaughan echoes eternal heartbreak,
but where there is heartbreak,
there was once love
swooping in without apologies or abandon
& when she speaks
violets spill onto asphalt
& she remembers that love is always
worth everything
& sleet melts into tulips
& love blooms again
on the cusp of the eclipse

My Favorite Things

Violet spilled moonlight
& opal etched silver
Santa Ana amethyst
& rain soaked Azaleas
Mt Rainer shrouded in fog,
These are a few of my favorite things

Secret staircases
& orchids at midnight
cerulean sunsets
& Wisteria swept doorways.
Cherry Blossoms rust
rustled dust.
These are a few of my favorite things.

The moon in her eyes
love on his lips.
Labyrinths & Labradorite
& Beethovens sweet symphonies.
These are a few of my favorite things.

888

I saw the number 888
spray painted
on a beater bronco
parked right beside me,
rockin a red rimmed spare tire.

I feel like you can really tell
how a person's doing
by the state of their tires,
& the conditions of their shoe soles.

I am deeply concerned
for the car parked on my left,
the wheel rim missing,
lug nuts exposed to elements,
the tread worn impossibly thin.

I feel like that tire most days;
worn down and thin
heat stretched rubber
melted into road,
metal parts exposed.

I hold onto hope
in the 888

spray painted
on the beater bronco
beside me.
Thank you for providing
sanctuary and solace
in this eternal moment.
There is a song
in my smoothie straw,
wind whistled wonder,
the wanderer searches
for water in the Desert of Spirit.

River Soliloquy!
I am learning to listen to wind,
hear the rustle whistle whisper of Spirit.
Spirit shine into me
like sunlight on rose quartz,
translucent, see through pink
sink into me.

I hear the whisper in thistle,
Muses sweet shimmer
eye corner glimmer,
the ecstasy of absolutely everything.

Lighthouse

Wild butterfly storm
let light root you

Poets Bookshop

Orchids bloom in the moonlight,
ochre seance,
eclipse,
sanctuary.
The Poets Portal opens
& love pours in.
Lost in the ether of the Muse,
linger in the ethereal river.
Elysian dust,
we sink into the Emerald Unknown
of crushed diamonds
& clove smoked embers.

Eclipse

Crescent sun,
orange sea,
fire scythe.
Kiss me in the Eclipse,
Rumi on my lips.
Heaven green forever.
The light dims,
a perfect circle.
Dance barefoot in the Eclipse,
in the space between ellipsis.
Sister,
lay down in the grass,
the light is beautiful,
eerie & iridescent
& electrically charged
celestial madness,
I am energized
in the spirit of love.
In the shadow of the eclipse,
there is love
only love
& the birds chip & chitter
in the false twilight,
the false night
& everything is aligning

in love in me.
Say yes quickly!
Yes Yes!
In the Eclipse.
Yes, Yes...

Invisible Ink

The calligraphy of crushed light
transforms illusions
& my Souls chandelier
is cobwebbed, dusty & old
the light is too dim.
Violets & ravens,
she slips into shadows
& orchids bloom in moonlight.
Butterfly wings cover her eyes
& the world flits away into dreams.

In the Center of the Eclipse

In the center of the eclipse
there is love
only love
& I will lie in the light
& shadow of love forever .
He walked through the eclipse.
Do I sleep?
Do I dream?
Dare I do to dream,
to anchor in holy light.
Daffodils die
as Hydrangeas bloom blue.
Underwater sunrise,
the eye of Atlantis, opens.